The G… of

…e

Killer Bugs

SCIENCE AGAINST AN INVISIBLE ENEMY

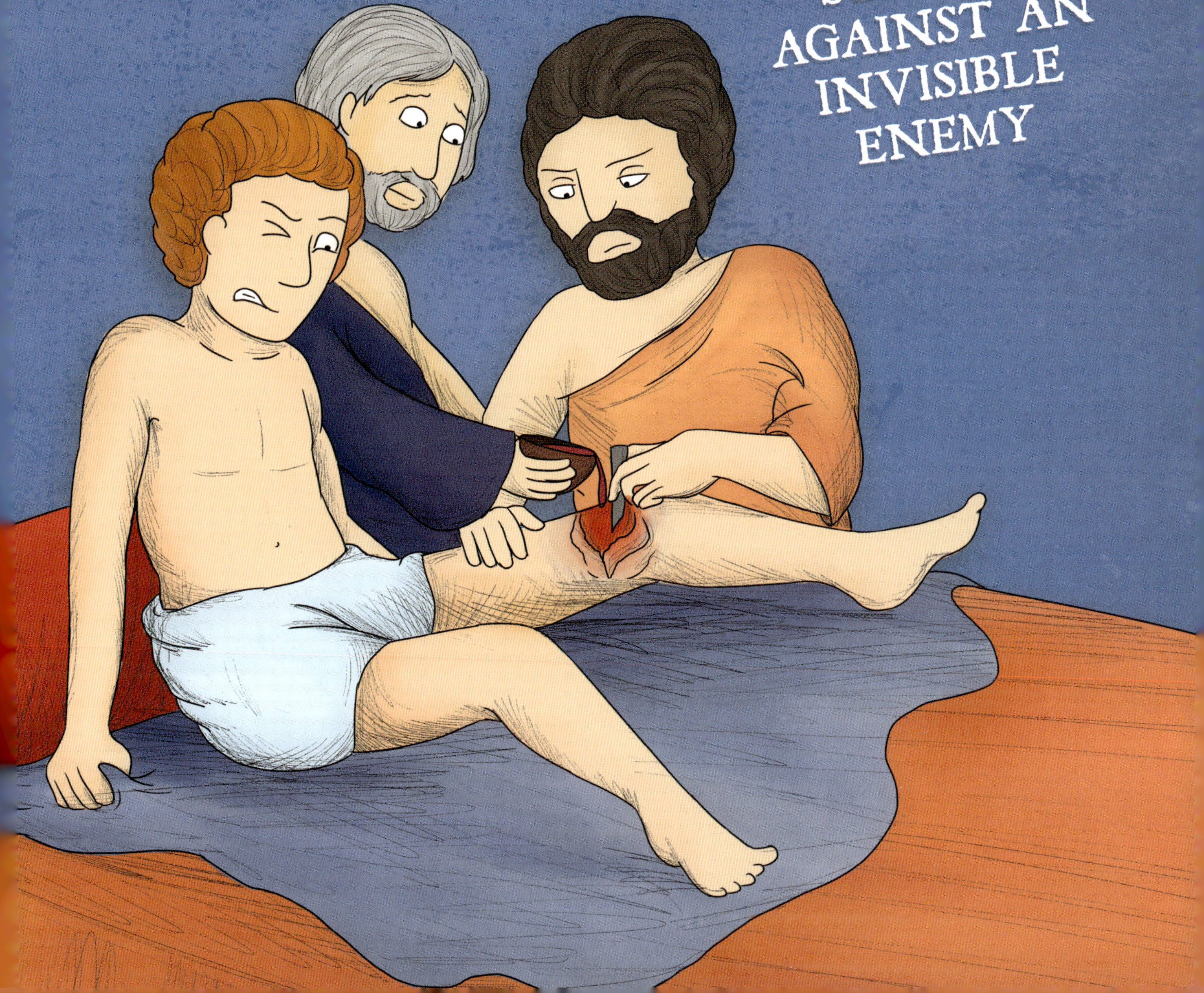

Thanks to the creative team:

Senior Editor: Alice Peebles
Editor: Angela Koo
Fact Checking: Kate Mitchell

Design: www.collaborate.agency

First published in Great Britain in 2016
by Hungry Tomato Ltd
PO Box 181
Edenbridge
Kent, TN8 9DP

A CIP catalogue record for this book is available from the British Library.

ISBN 978-1-910684-62-7

Printed and bound in China

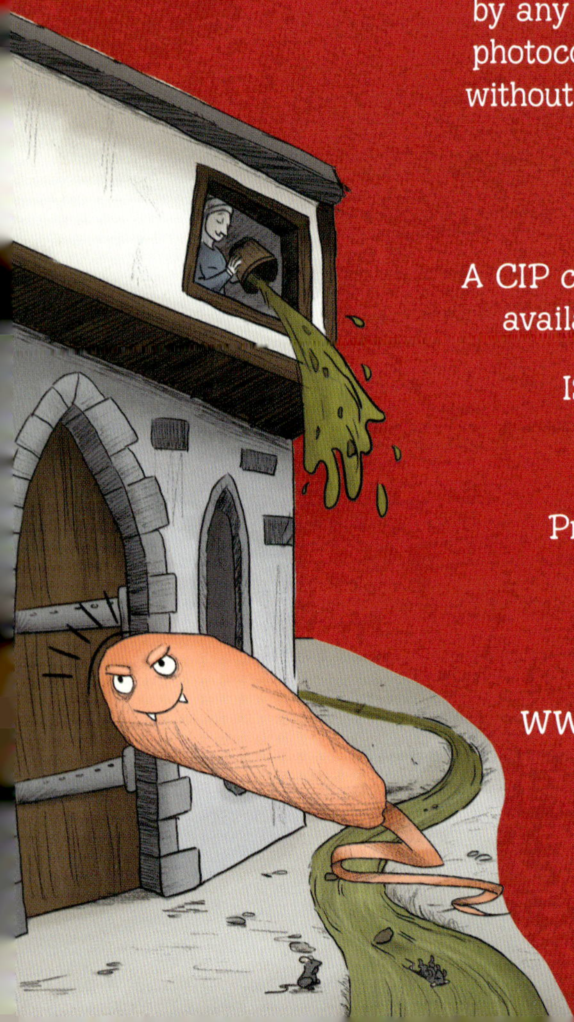

Discover more at
www.hungrytomato.com

The Grisly History of
Medicine

Killer Bugs

By John Farndon
Illustrated by Venitia Dean

HUNGRY TOMATO

Contents

INTRODUCTION

Germs are tiny organisms, living things, that make you sick. Because they're far too small to see, they sneak into your body without you noticing and then infect you with all kinds of terrible diseases. This book tells the story of how these microscopic monsters were finally unmasked...

Home wreckers

Germs don't actually try to make us ill. It's just that bodies like ours make very good homes for them, and once they get inside, they multiply rapidly to make the most of their good luck! That's how they do the damage.

Catching germs

Germs are found all over the world, in all kinds of places. Some reach you through the air via sneezes, coughs or someone's breath. You can also become infected if you touch somewhere contaminated with germs, then touch your nose and breathe in. Other germs can be swallowed when you eat bad food.

Defenders

Luckily, your body has an amazing defence system for dealing with germs called the 'immune system'. It's a complex army of tiny cells that circulate in your blood and do battle with germs. It often takes time to kick in, though. That's why you get ill – then, with luck, recover because your immune system has dealt with them.

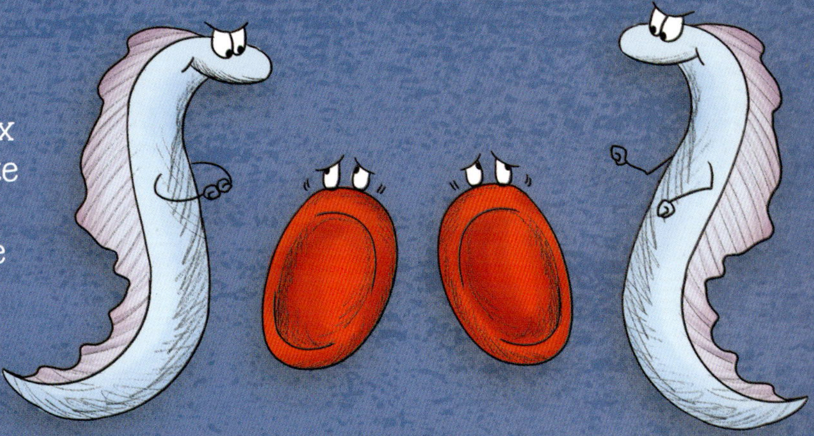

Doctor's orders

Doctors have two ways of helping your body fight germs. One is with vaccination, which primes your body's immune system to fight particular germs. The other is with antibiotics – chemicals that you usually swallow in pills – which are poisonous to germs.

Keeping clean

There's another way we can reduce the danger of germs – by cleanliness, or 'hygiene'. Many germs spread in dirt, so by keeping things clean we reduce the chances of infection. That's why it's good to wash your hands.

SETTLING FOR GERMS

In the early days of mankind, when people roamed around hunting and gathering, infectious diseases were probably rare. People did not live close enough together for germs to spread, or stay long enough near water sources to pollute them.

Disease on the farm

The development of farming some 10,000 years ago saved mankind from starvation and provided food for the first towns and cities. But we now know that germs multiplied as people and farm animals began living close together, sharing their germs, and water became polluted.

The first known polio victim?

On an Egyptian monument from the 13th century BCE, there is a picture of a man called Roma. He seems to have a withered leg, which could be caused by polio. If so, he is the first known victim of this terrible disease, which may have developed in water dirtied by the dung of farm animals.

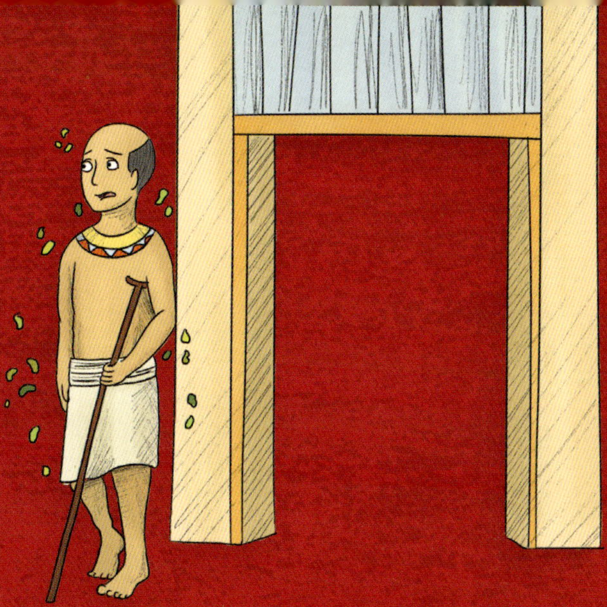

As farming became more intense, manure-polluted water encouraged diseases such as polio, cholera, typhoid and hepatitis. Slow-moving irrigation water provided ideal conditions for parasites such as those causing the diseases bilharzia and malaria.

BAD AIR

Few people had any idea diseases were spread by tiny invisible germs. Most thought bad, smelly air was to blame – especially damp, misty air near ditches and swamps. This nasty mist was called a 'miasma'.

Dealing with odours

Most people in ancient India, as elsewhere in the world, thought disease was caused by poisonous air. They chewed a paste made from the leaves of the gambir tree as an antidote.

Morning smells

The Roman writer Vitruvius was convinced it was a very bad idea to build a city anywhere near swamps. He believed morning breezes would blow miasmas from the marshes, along with the poisonous breath of swamp creatures, to the city and make people ill.

Taking it on the Ch'in

Government officials in ancient China knew they were in trouble if they were sent off to the south! The Ch'in Mountains there were damp and misty, and people were convinced that poisonous air would make them fall ill and die.

Smoke in New Orleans

The city of New Orleans often suffered from outbreaks of disease. People were convinced this was because of bad air full of evil spirits coming from the nearby swamps. So they burned huge bonfires of feverfew plants and fired cannons into the air to keep the evil mist at bay.

The Great Stink

In the past, so much sewage poured into the River Thames in London that in the hot summer of 1858, the stink coming off it was bad enough to make you throw up. They called it the Great Stink and people began to leave the city – convinced the terrible smell of sewage gas caused deadly disease. To solve the problem, London built the first modern sewage system.

EASTERN IDEAS

You might think people had no idea about germs in the past because they are just too small to see. But in India more than 2,500 years ago, those who followed the Jainist religion were taught that tiny life forms called 'nigoda' existed all around them.

Saving germs

Just as people nowadays often wear surgical masks in order not to breathe in germs, so did the Jains, thousands of years ago. But their aim was not to avoid disease. They believed they must not harm any living thing, and wanted to avoid killing the tiny nigoda by accidentally swallowing them!

Ancient medicine

Ayurveda is an ancient medical system, developed in India more than 3,000 years ago, that uses complex mixes of herbs to treat people. Scientists are not sure if it works, but many people still use it. But Ayurvedists believed more than 2,000 years ago that microbes cause diseases such as leprosy and meningitis.

Prevention better than cure

The most famous old book of Ayurvedic medicine was the *Charaka Samhita,* written about 2,200 years ago by Charaka. He argued that prevention is better than cure. That's why he suggested different diets to keep you healthy in different places and at different times of year.

The plague in Granada

In 1350, the bubonic plague reached Granada in Spain, then part of the Islamic world. Physician Ibn Khatima suggested it was spread by 'minute bodies', which sound rather like germs. Another physician, al-Khatib – shown in the orange headscarf with the Vizier (ruler) in Granada's Alhambra Palace – explained how such organisms spread the plague by contact between people.

INVISIBLE ANIMALS

Around 1590, Dutch spectacle maker Zacharias Janssen put some lenses together – and invented the microscope. When people began to look through it, they were blown away by what they saw: a whole new unknown world of tiny organisms, too small to see normally.

Hooked in

In 1665, the English physicist Robert Hooke (1635–1703) published *Micrographia,* a book full of drawings of the amazing things he viewed down a microscope – things people had never seen before. In slices of cork, he could see a honeycomb network of boxes. He called the boxes 'cells', and we now know all living things are built up from tiny cells.

Tiny monsters

Dutch scientist Anton van Leeuwenhoek (1632–1723) made a microscope with just a single lens. It was simple but brilliant, and he could see things 200 times larger than life! He discovered that clear water is not clear at all, but teeming with tiny creatures. In fact, there are tiny creatures almost everywhere.

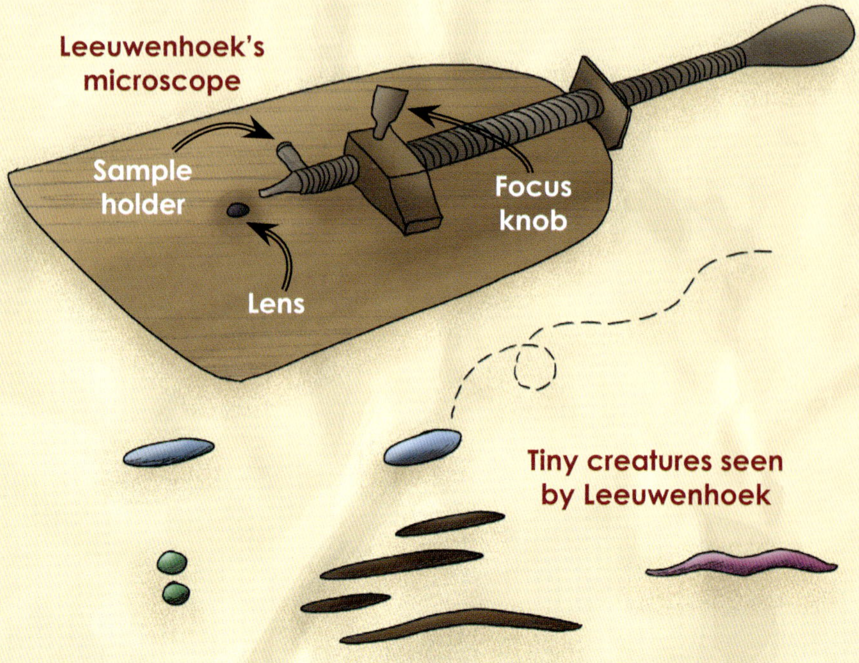

Germs spotted

Leeuwenhoek was astonished by the range of creatures he saw (above). Many looked like monsters. It was Leeuwenhoek who saw germs for the first time, when he looked through his microscope at the bacteria wriggling in plaque taken from his wife's and daughter's teeth.

The bacteria four

After Leeuwenhoek's great discovery, no one paid much attention to bacteria for the next 200 years, until German biologist Ferdinand Cohn began to study them closely in the 1870s. Cohn realized that, though there are many kinds of bacteria, they can be divided into four groups, depending on their shape: spheres, rods, threads and spirals.

Spheres

Rods

Threads

Spirals

NOW WASH YOUR HANDS

Hospitals in the past were deadly dangerous! Very few people knew that germs caused disease, so doctors and nurses spread diseases as they went from patient to patient, with terrible consequences.

Don't take me to the hospital!

Giving birth at home was never easy for young mums. But hospitals were deadly. Doctors carried the killer childbed or 'puerperal' fever on their hands, and spread it from one young mum to the next. So going into hospital to give birth could be a death sentence!

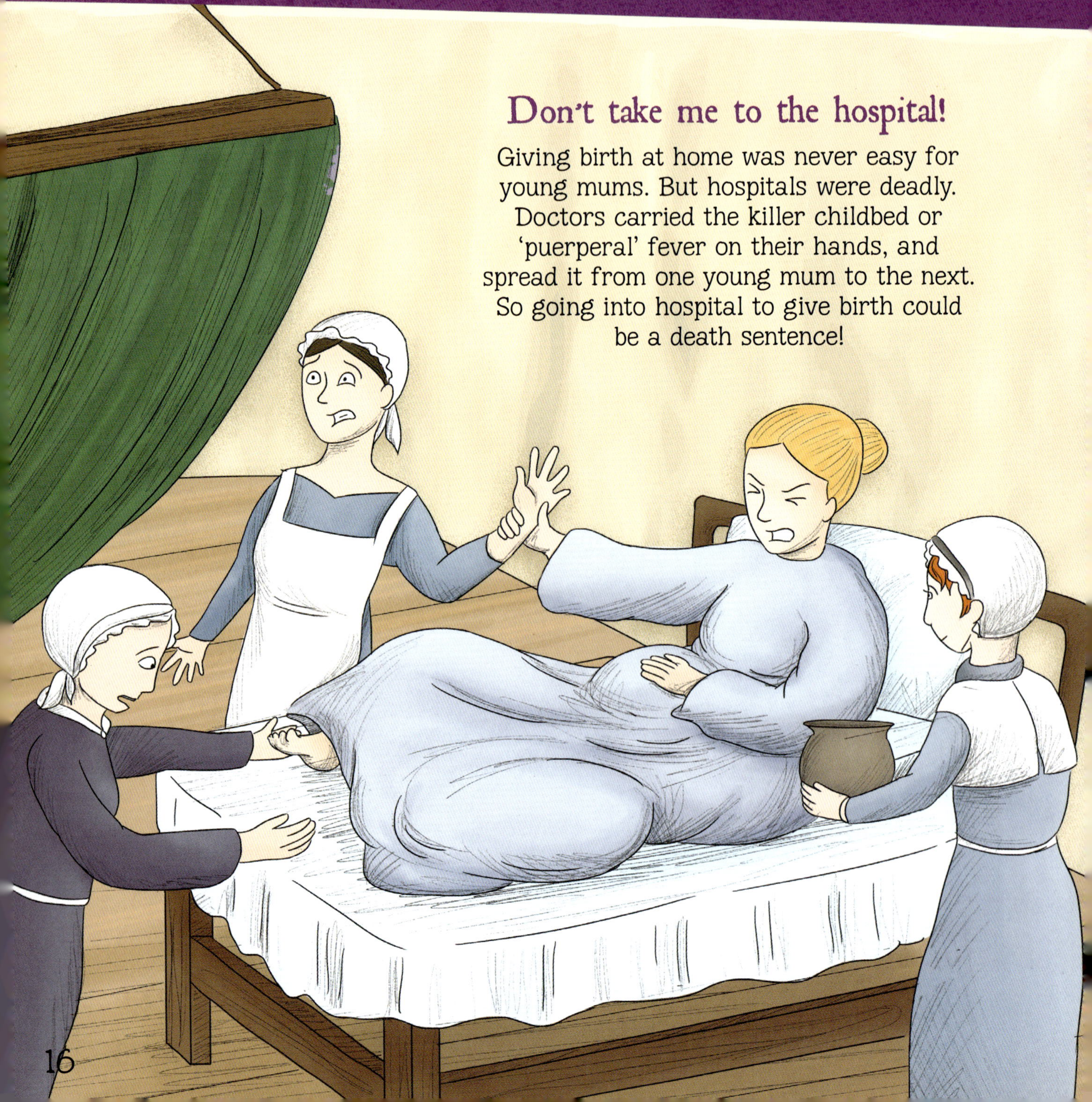

The real culprit

Of course, the doctors weren't really to blame. Their unwashed hands were simply carrying the germs that were the real culprits. As we now know, the germ that causes childbed fever is the bacterium *Streptococcus pyogenes*. Fortunately, proper hygiene in hospitals means this germ very rarely has its evil way!

Trust me, I'm a doctor!

In Vienna General Hospital in the 1800s, doctors often handled diseased corpses in the mortuary, then nipped next door to Maternity Ward 1 to examine mums-to-be – with fatal results. When the young Hungarian doctor Ignaz Semmelweis (1818–65) arrived in 1847, he was appalled by the high death rate on the ward – and realized the doctors were to blame.

My hands are clean

Semmelweis ordered all medical staff to wash their hands regularly in calcium chloride. At once, death rates on Maternity Ward 1 dropped. But doctors could not believe they were to blame. They sacked Semmelweis, and carried on as before. It was a while before everyone realized just how important cleanliness, or 'hygiene', is in stopping germs spreading.

DIRTY DRAINS

In the 1800s, London and other European cities grew rapidly – and so did deaths from the killer disease cholera. Poor people were especially hard hit by cholera.

Feeling blue

Cholera is a horrible disease that seems to have originated in India on the banks of the River Ganges. Victims may suffer from diarrhoea so severe that their bodies are drained of water. Their eyes go hollow, their skin shrivels and they turn blue.

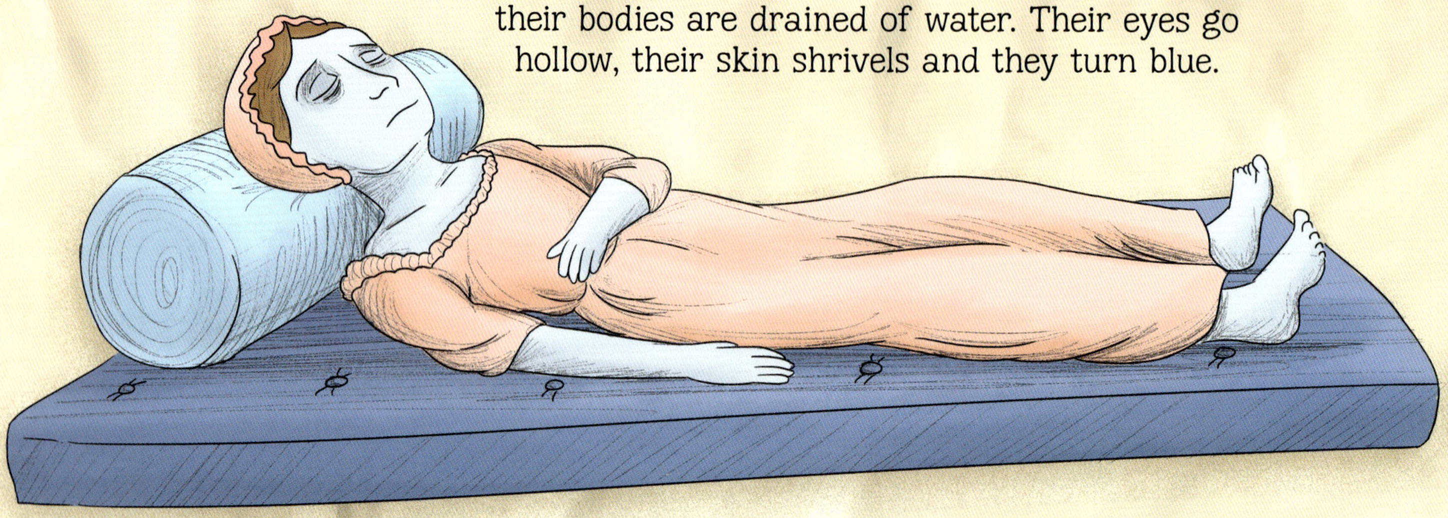

Where's that smell?

Experts in the past were convinced that cholera was spread by miasmas. So for the upper class, it was obviously smelly poor people who were to blame! A cartoon of the time pokes fun at health officials trying to sniff out just where the worst stinks were coming from.

The Soho pump

English doctor John Snow didn't think the miasma theory was right. When cholera hit London's Soho district in 1854, he found that all the victims had drunk water from just one pump in Broadwick Street. Human poo had contaminated the water supply for the pump. But it was a while before people understood that cholera is caused by germs in dirty water.

The fast way to travel

The opening of Egypt's Suez Canal in 1869 cut the sea journey from India to Europe dramatically – and made it much easier for cholera epidemics to spread. London escaped the worst because by then it had built good sewers, but many other European cities suffered badly.

Vicious Vibrion

In 1854, cholera hit Florence in Italy, the same year that it hit London's Soho. In Florence, Dr Filippo Pacini looked down his microscope and identified the culprit: the bacterium *Vibrio cholerae*. But everyone ignored him, since they thought miasmas were to blame. Then in 1884, German doctor Robert Koch, too, nailed *Vibrio* as the cause of cholera – and he was so famous that everyone believed him!

GUILTY GERMS

In the 1840s and '50s, Semmelweis and Snow showed how clean hands and good drains could cut the spread of disease. So how could bad air be to blame? Then in the 1860s, the French microbiologist Louis Pasteur began to demonstrate that the real culprits are germs – also known as microbes.

Life from nothing

When people saw maggots crawling from rotten apples or dead meat, it didn't occur to them the maggots had hatched from eggs. They thought they simply appeared whenever food rotted. This idea of life appearing from nothing is known as 'spontaneous generation'.

Life from the air

In 1859, Pasteur (1822–95) demonstrated with a simple experiment that microbes won't appear magically by spontaneous generation when food decays. Instead, they fall from the air on dust.

1. Pasteur boiled meat broth in a flask with a bent 'swan' neck to kill off any microbes.

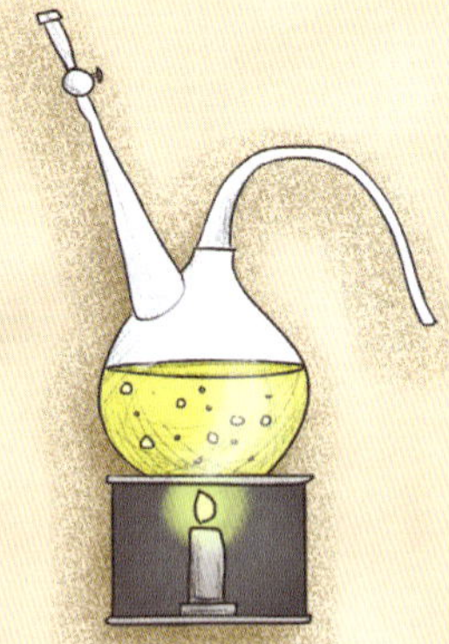

2. The swan neck stopped dust falling in, so the broth stayed clear.

3. He then broke off the neck to allow dust to fall in. The broth quickly went cloudy, showing microbes were multiplying.

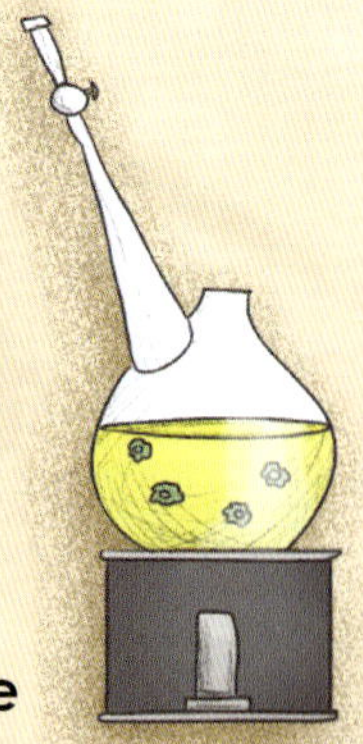

Germs on worms

In 1867, Pasteur showed that germs can cause disease. He had been studying a disease that was killing silkworms, the caterpillars that make silk. When Pasteur examined the diseased worms through his microscope, he found they were infected by not just one kind of microbe, but two.

Chicken test

In 1880, Pasteur discovered how to protect people against germs with experiments on chickens. He grew chicken cholera germs in a dish, then starved them of nutrition so they became weak. When he injected chickens with these old germs, the chickens became immune to the disease. Vaccinating people with weakened germs is now one of the main ways of preventing diseases.

Sheep shot

In 1881, Pasteur also found a way to weaken the germs that cause anthrax in sheep. Using these weak germs, he vaccinated sheep so that they became immune to anthrax.

GERMS NAILED

Louis Pasteur proved there are germs, or microbes, in the air, and that they can cause disease. Then Robert Koch showed there's a whole army of nasty microbes out there – and that it's these nasty microbes that are to blame for most diseases.

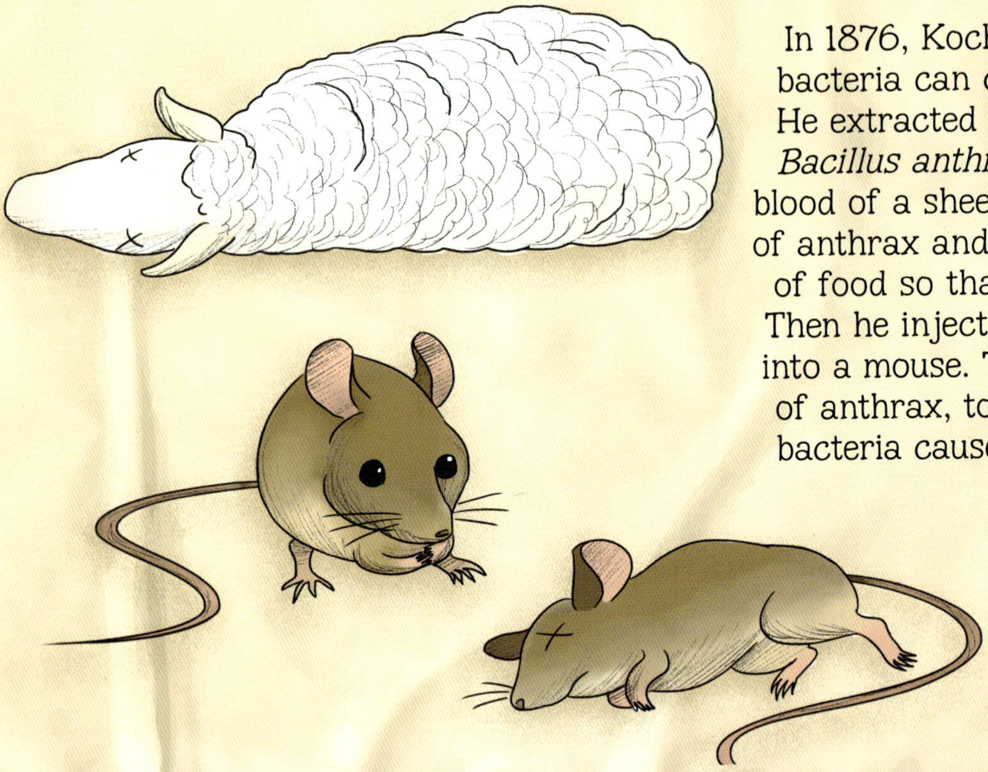

Guilty!

In 1876, Koch proved that bacteria can cause disease. He extracted the bacterium *Bacillus anthracis* from the blood of a sheep that had died of anthrax and put it in a dish of food so that it multiplied. Then he injected the bacteria into a mouse. The mouse died of anthrax, too, proving the bacteria caused the disease.

The criminal

Bacillus anthracis is a rod-shaped organism. It's so tiny you can only see it under a microscope. But despite its small size, it can kill a sheep or even a person. It does its damage by multiplying dramatically in the body and releasing a poison.

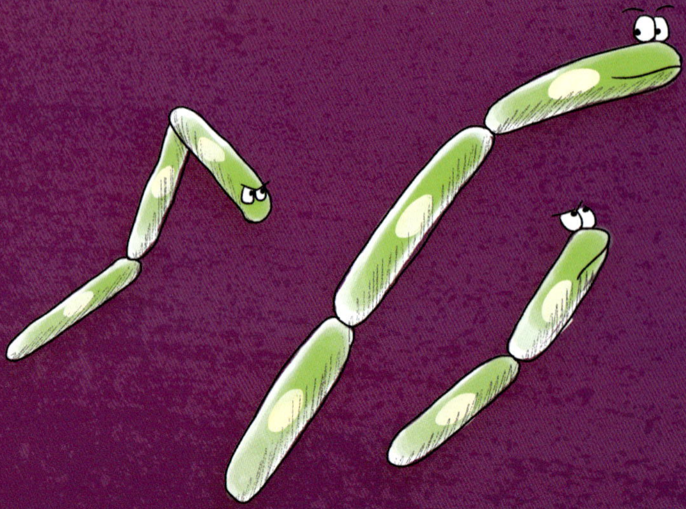

Cultured germs

Koch's work with germs depended on growing them in a dish in the laboratory. Growths like this are called 'cultures', and they need food. At first, Koch used the liquid from an ox's eye as food for germ cultures. Later he developed a broth of agar (a jelly made from algae) and gelatine (a jelly made from animal bones).

The four tests

Koch's work led him to establish four tests for proving which germ causes a disease.

1. Association: the germ and the disease are seen together all the time.

2. Isolation: the germ can be taken from the diseased animal and grown in a culture.

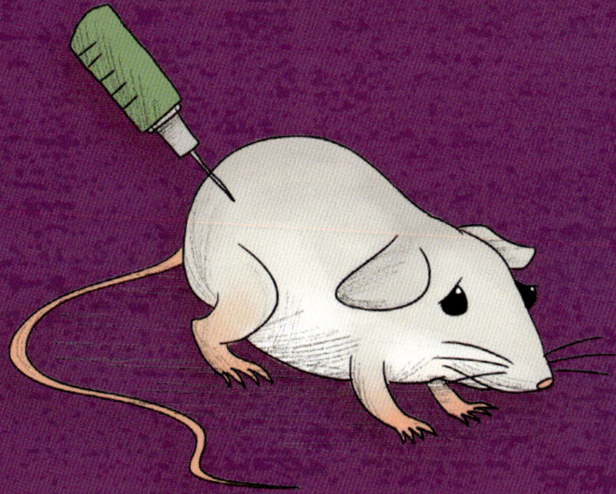

3. Inoculation: the germ taken from the diseased animal causes the disease in a healthy animal.

4. Re-isolation: the germ can also be taken from the newly infected animal.

CLEAN SURGERY

If germs cause disease, how do we stop them? One answer is to keep clean. Semmelweis showed how important it was to keep clean when mothers gave birth. British surgeon Joseph Lister showed how vital it was for surgery.

Mummy, you're rotten

Dead bodies rot away because they are attacked by microbes. But the Ancient Egyptians learned how to stop the rot by turning the bodies into mummies. This meant soaking the body in 'embalming fluids' that were poisonous to microbes.

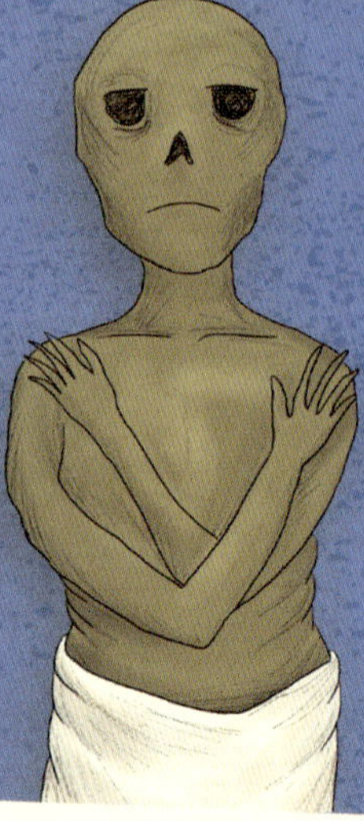

Pus is bad

The 13th-century surgeon Hugh of Lucca realized the dangers of wounds becoming infected and so he cleaned them with wine. He knew that pus oozing from a wound was a bad sign, showing the wound was infected. Most doctors at the time thought (wrongly) that pus was a sign that the wound was getting better.

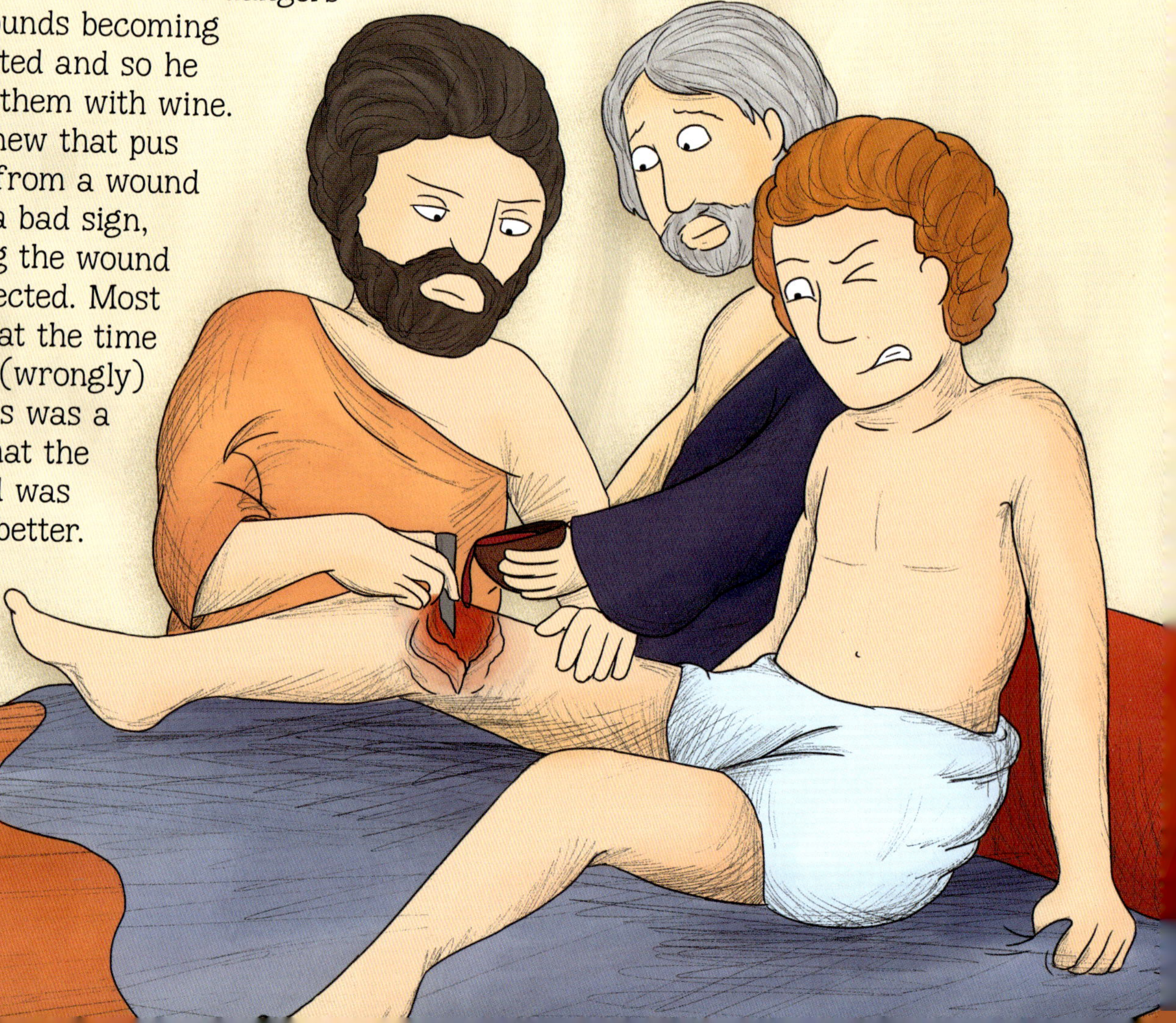

Filth

The growing cities of the 1800s were filthy places, because they had no proper rubbish collection, a poor water supply and a lack of good drains. In such conditions, germs could spread easily. Hospitals were among the worst culprits for germ-friendly filth!

Clean surgery

Until the 1860s, all too many patients undergoing surgery died of infections afterwards. Then Joseph Lister (1827–1912) introduced the idea of 'antiseptic' surgery. He made sure that hands, instruments and surfaces were thoroughly washed with germ-killing chemicals such as carbolic soap. The idea worked, and now it is standard practice around the world.

Masked doctors

Lister's antiseptic methods stopped the spread of germs from surface to surface. But germs could still spread through the air. The answer was simple – surgeons and other surgical staff needed to wear masks that sieve germs from their breath and stop them infecting patients.

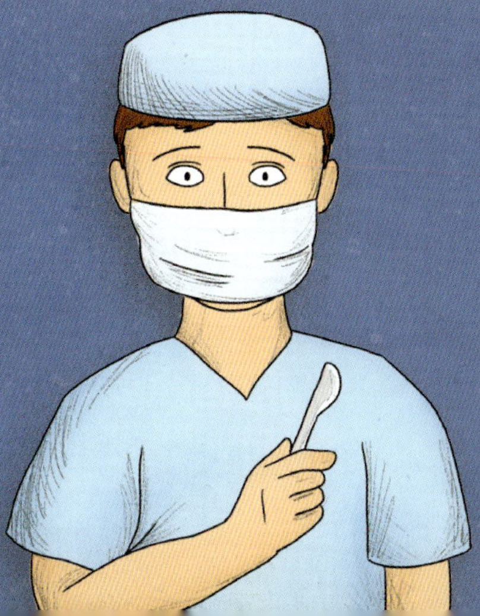

GERM ARMY

Although 99 per cent of microbes are completely harmless, scientists have now identified about 1,500 that can make you ill. They call these disease-causing microbes, or germs, 'pathogens'. The main kinds are viruses, fungi, protozoa and bacteria. Here is a round-up of some of these tiny villains.

Viruses

Viruses are much tinier than any other kind of germ. They only come to life once they have invaded and taken over a living cell, such as one of your body cells.

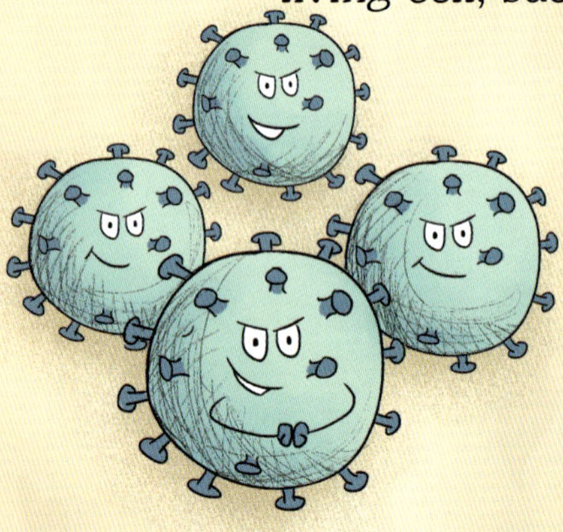

Influenza viruses give you colds and flu. Type C gives you minor colds, type B gives you winter flu, and type A bird flu.

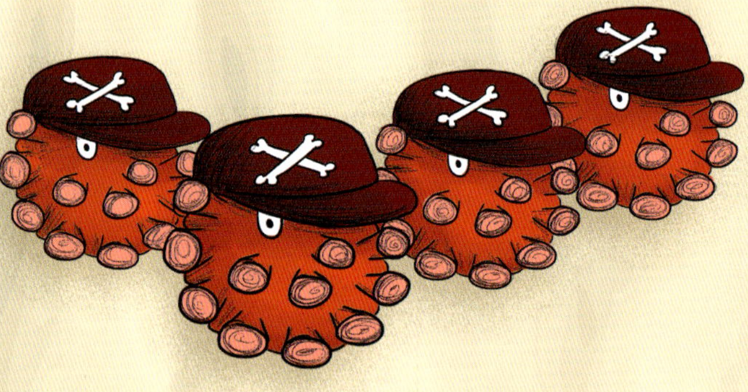

The togavirus causes rubella (German measles).

Adenoviruses give rise to sore throats, colds, bronchitis, conjunctivitis, diarrhoea and pneumonia.

The human immuno-deficiency virus (HIV) causes AIDS.

Fungi and protozoa

A few diseases are caused by tiny organisms called fungi and protozoa.

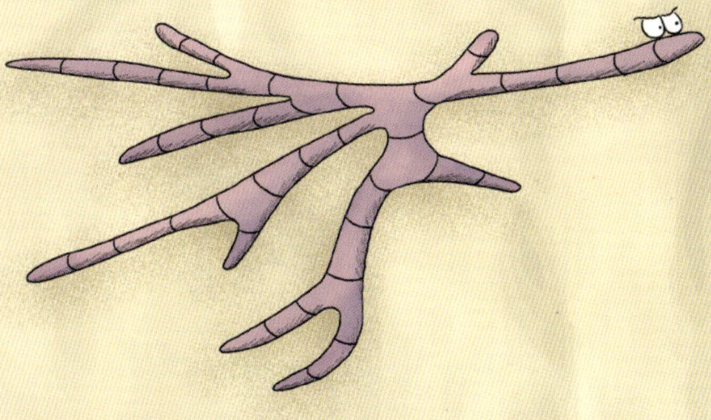

Fungi can cause skin infections such as athlete's foot.

The protozoa *Trypanosoma brucei* causes sleeping sickness by attacking red blood cells.

Bacteria

Bacteria are tiny microbes made from just one cell. Most are harmless, but a few are germs that make you ill.

Bacilli are long, thin and rod-like, and cause tetanus (lockjaw), typhoid, tuberculosis (TB), whooping cough and diphtheria. Not welcome!

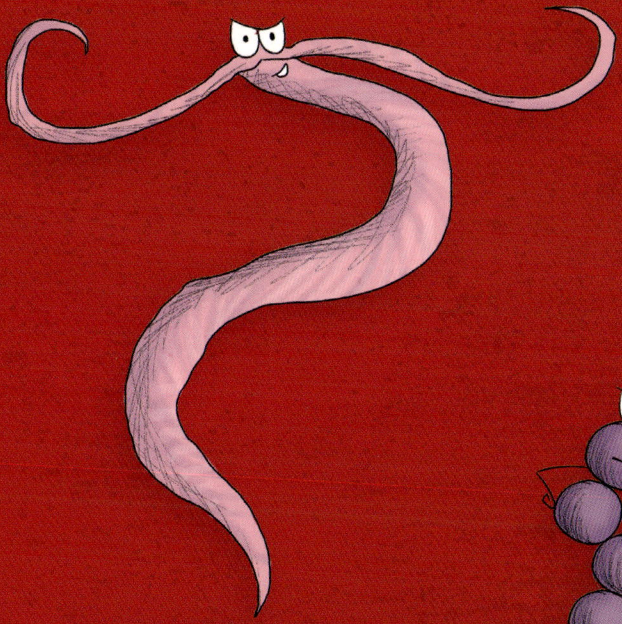

Spirilla look like tiny spiral pasta noodles and cause diarrhoea and stomach upsets.

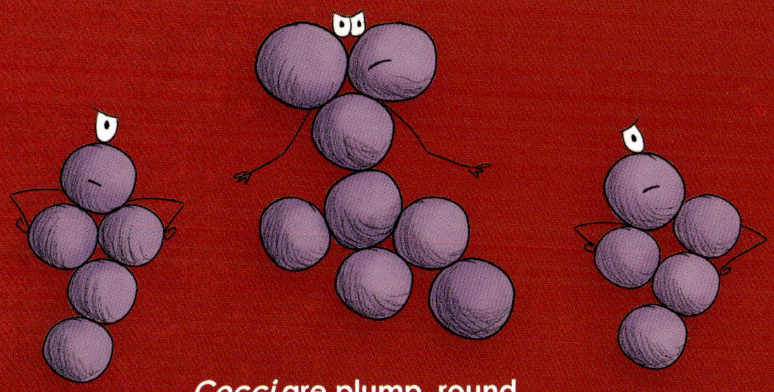

Cocci are plump, round bacteria that cause strep throat, pneumonia, scarlet fever and meningitis.

GERMY TIMES

Some people suspected that germs caused disease long ago. Here are some of the key steps on the way to the discovery of just what germs are, and how they make you ill.

1665
Microscopic cells

English scientist Robert Hooke saw through a microscope that living things are made from tiny boxes, or 'cells'.

Around 1000 BCE
Old herbalists

In India, the Ayurvedic system of medicine suggested that many diseases were caused by tiny microbes.

1546
The seeds of disease

Italian physician Girolamo Fracastoro suggested that diseases are spread far and wide by tiny seeds.

1676 Viewing bacteria

Dutch scientist Anton van Leeuwenhoek was the first person to see bacteria, through a homemade microscope.

1847 Hygiene

Hungarian doctor Ignaz Semmelweis cut dangerous infections among mothers giving birth simply by getting all medical staff to wash their hands.

1859 Germs in the air

French scientist Louis Pasteur proved that there are microbes in the air that might cause disease.

1870s Antiseptic surgery

Surgeon Joseph Lister showed how keeping everything completely clean stopped germs spreading and patients dying from infection after surgery.

1750

1860

1876 Germs cause disease

German doctor Robert Koch proved that a particular bacterium caused the disease anthrax.

1854 Sanitation

London doctor John Snow showed that cholera was spread not by bad vapours but by sewage-contaminated water.

1890s Germ theory

Following on from Koch's ideas, scientists developed the germ theory: the idea that a small range of micro-organisms, known as pathogens or germs, are the cause of all infectious diseases.

GRUESOME SYMPTOMS

One species of bacterium is so resistant to radiation that scientists have nicknamed it 'Conan the Bacterium'.

When you cough, germs can travel about three metres (10 ft) if you don't cover your nose or mouth with your hand or a handkerchief.

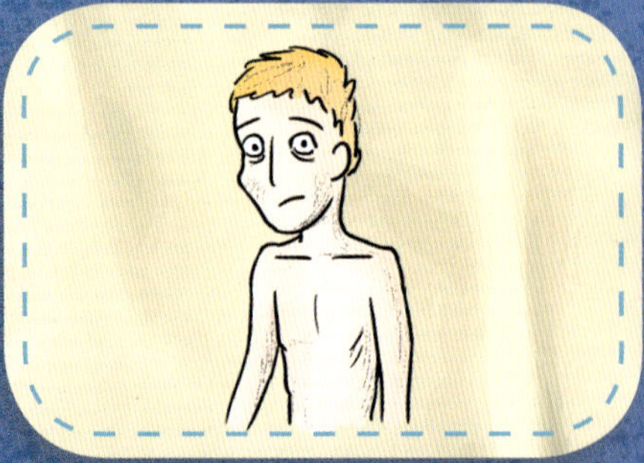

There are more bacteria on your skin than there are people in the world. Take out the water, and a tenth of your body weight is bacteria.

Bacteria in your nose and mouth are what give you bad breath.

Poo, by weight, is mostly bacteria.

The average kitchen sink contains 100,000 times more germs than the bathroom.

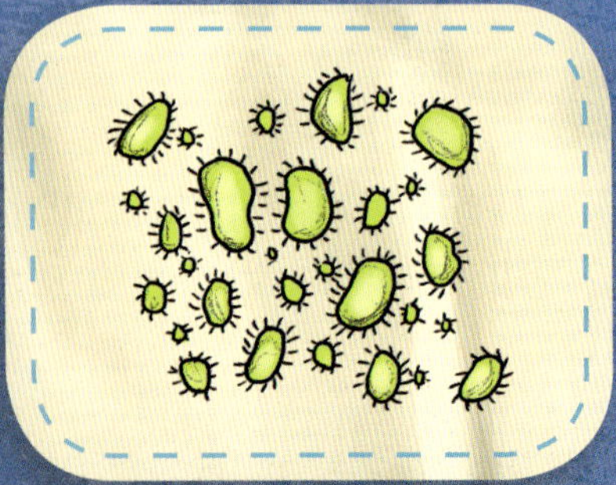

Bacteria double in number every 20 minutes. A single bacterium could divide and multiply into trillions in just one day, if all the bacteria survived.

Some soldiers in the American Civil War had 'glow-in-the-dark' wounds because of a bioluminescent bacteria that was puked up by nematode worms.

When you flush a toilet, an invisible cloud of water full of germs shoots far up into the air.

GLOSSARY

Antidote	A remedy for counteracting the effects of a poison or a germ.
Antiseptic	A substance wiped or sprayed on surfaces to kill germs.
Ayurveda	An ancient medical system developed in India that treats people with complex mixes of herbs.
Bacteria	(singular: bacterium) Invisibly small living things made from just a single cell. A few of them cause disease.
Bubonic plague	A dreadful disease caused by the *Yersinia pestis* bacterium that often causes distinctive buboes (blisters).
Epidemic	A widespread outbreak of an infectious disease.
Germ	A microbe that causes disease when it enters the body.
Hygiene	Cleanliness that reduces the spread of infection.
Immune system	The body's microscopic defences against germs.
Inoculation	The use of germs to stimulate the body's immune system to guard against infection.
Miasma	A damp, smelly mist that was believed to spread disease.
Microbe	A microscopic living thing, especially one that causes diseases, such as a bacterium.
Puerperal fever	A disease that affects mothers giving birth, also known as childbed fever.
Vaccination	The use of dead or inactivated germs to stimulate the body's immune system to guard against infection.
Virus	A tiny germ that reproduces only inside other living cells – including yours.

Index

The Author

John Farndon is the author of many books on science, technology and nature, including the international best-sellers *Do Not Open* and *Do You Think You're Clever?* He has been shortlisted six times for the British Royal Society's Young People's Book Prize for a science book.

The Illustrator

Venitia Dean grew up in Brighton, UK. She has loved drawing ever since she could hold a pencil. After receiving a digital drawing tablet for her 19th birthday she transferred to working digitally. She hasn't looked back since!

BBQ Baby Back Ribs

GLUTEN FREE • DAIRY FREE • SOY FREE • NUT FREE • EGG FREE

1 (3-pound, or 1.4 kg) rack of baby back ribs

2 tablespoons (30 g) brown sugar

1 tablespoon (6 g) smoked paprika

1 tablespoon (6 g) chili powder (Penzeys and McCormick brands clearly mark their products for allergens)

1 tablespoon (18 g) kosher or fine sea salt

2 teaspoons (1 g) dried thyme leaves

2 teaspoons (2 g) onion powder (*not* onion salt)

1 teaspoon garlic powder (*not* garlic salt)

1 teaspoon freshly ground black pepper

Your favorite gluten-free barbecue sauce (Stubb's brand is gluten free)

For the cooking pot

1¼ cups (295 ml) water

—

2 to 3 servings

Lay the ribs bone side up on a baking sheet and remove the membrane covering the surface. Place the trivet in the bottom of the inner pot and pour in the water.

In a small bowl, mix together the brown sugar, smoked paprika, chili powder, salt, thyme, onion powder, garlic powder, and pepper. Rub the seasoning mix over all sides of the ribs. Stand the ribs around the edges of the inner pot.

Close and lock the lid, making sure the steam release handle is in the sealing position. Cook on high pressure for 17 minutes. When it is finished, release the pressure naturally for 10 minutes, then move the handle to venting and release the remaining steam. Unlock the lid and open it carefully. Press Cancel.

Use tongs to transfer the ribs to a clean baking sheet. Preheat the broiler. Lightly brush one side of the ribs with barbecue sauce. Slide the ribs under the broiler for a few minutes until the sauce is bubbling. Flip the pieces over and repeat the broiling, brushing with more sauce. Watch carefully so the ribs don't burn.

Serve while hot, passing additional sauce at the table.

Sensational Side Dishes

Recipes

Green Bean Casserole with Fried Onions
(page 94)

Steamed Broccoli with Cheese Sauce

GLUTEN FREE • SOY FREE • NUT FREE • EGG FREE

FOR THE BROCCOLI

2½ cups (175 g) broccoli florets

1 tablespoon (15 ml) olive oil

2 teaspoons (6 g) minced garlic

1 teaspoon red pepper flakes

½ teaspoon salt

½ teaspoon black pepper

FOR THE CHEESE SAUCE

3 tablespoons (42 g) unsalted butter

3 tablespoons (24 g) rice flour

1¼ cups (295 ml) milk

2 teaspoons (4 g) garlic powder

1 teaspoon onion powder

1 cup (120 g) shredded sharp cheddar cheese

Salt, to taste (optional)

—

1½ cups (355 ml) cheese sauce, about 6 servings

BROCCOLI: In a large bowl, toss the broccoli florets with the olive oil, minced garlic, red pepper flakes, salt, and pepper. Place a steamer basket in the inner pot of your electric pressure cooker. Pour 1 cup (235 ml) water into the pot. Place the seasoned broccoli in the steamer basket.

Close and lock the lid, making sure the steam release handle is in the sealing position. Press Manual and cook on high pressure for 0 (zero) minutes.

When the cook time is finished, do a quick pressure release by carefully moving the sealing handle to venting and allowing all the steam to escape. When the float pin drops, unlock the lid and open it carefully.

Remove the cooked broccoli to a large bowl. Cover with aluminum foil and set aside.

CHEESE SAUCE: Remove the steamer basket from your pressure cooker and dump out the water. Wipe the pot dry and return to the housing unit. Press Sauté and add the butter. When the butter is melted, whisk in the rice flour, whisk continuously so the resulting roux doesn't stick to the bottom or begin to brown. Cook for 1 minute. Slowly whisk in the milk and let simmer until it just begins to thicken, stirring continuously. Add the garlic and onion powders. Add the cheese, ½ cup (60 g) at a time, so it melts completely. Adjust the seasonings if necessary.

Serve the cheese sauce over the steamed broccoli.

Quick and Easy Potato Salad

GLUTEN FREE • SOY FREE, NUT FREE

4 medium russet potatoes (or red potatoes), peeled and cubed (approximately 3½ cups, or 385 g)

3 eggs

¾ cup (180 g) mayonnaise

1 teaspoon paprika

1 teaspoon onion salt

1 teaspoon garlic powder

¼ teaspoon cracked black pepper

1 tablespoon (11 g) spicy mustard

3 tablespoons (45 g) sweet pickle relish

2 stalks celery, diced

Salt and pepper, to taste

—

6 servings

Add 1 cup (235 ml) water to your inner cooking pot. Place a steamer basket over the water.

Place the potatoes and whole eggs in the steamer basket, nestling the eggs in with the potatoes.

Close and lock the lid, making sure the steam release handle is in the sealing position. Cook on high pressure for 5 minutes. When the cook time is finished, do a quick release by carefully moving the sealing handle to venting and allowing all the steam to escape. When the float pin drops, unlock the lid and open it carefully.

Remove the eggs to a bowl of ice water and let cool for 6 minutes.

Remove the potatoes to a large bowl to cool slightly. Once the potatoes are cool, add the mayonnaise, spices, mustard, relish, and celery to the bowl. Stir to combine.

Peel the shells from the eggs. Chop the eggs and add them to the potato mixture. Taste and adjust the seasonings. Add additional mayonnaise if desired.

Chill for 1 hour before serving.

BBQ Baked Beans

GLUTEN FREE • SOY FREE • NUT FREE • DAIRY FREE • EGG FREE • VEGETARIAN OPTION

1 pound (454 g) dried navy beans (optional soaking for 8 to 12 hours)

6 strips thick-cut bacon, roughly diced (Applewood Farms is gluten free)

1 medium onion, roughly diced

3 cups (705 ml) water, divided

⅓ cup (105 g) molasses

¼ cup (60 ml) maple syrup

½ cup (120 ml) tomato sauce

⅓ cup (75 g) brown sugar

1 teaspoon liquid smoke (Wright's brand is gluten free)

2 teaspoons (6 g) dry mustard powder

1 teaspoon apple cider vinegar

¼ teaspoon salt

Ground black pepper, to taste

—

6 servings

NOTE:

To make your beans vegetarian, simply leave out the bacon!

Rinse and sort the navy beans, removing any stones or debris. If desired, add the beans to a bowl and cover with water to 2 inches (5 cm) above the beans. Soak for 8 hours or overnight. Drain the beans and rinse.

Press Sauté on your pressure cooker. When the inner pot is hot, add the bacon and cook until it begins to render. Don't let the bacon get too crisp. Add the onions to the pot with the bacon and continue to sauté until they begin to soften, 2 minutes. Add ¼ cup (60 ml) of the water to the pot and scrape up any brown bits from the bottom. Continue cooking until all the water has evaporated.

Add the drained beans and all the remaining ingredients to the pot. Stir well to combine.

Close and lock the lid, making sure the steam release handle is in the sealing position. Cook on high pressure for 60 minutes. When the cook time is finished, allow a 25-minute natural release, then do a quick release to vent any remaining steam. When the float pin drops, unlock the lid and open it carefully.

Discard any floating beans. Stir well. Taste a few beans for tenderness. If the beans are still hard, return the lid and cook on high pressure for another 15 minutes, with a 15-minute natural pressure release.

Once the beans are tender, taste again for sweetness and adjust the seasonings if desired. Add more molasses or brown sugar for sweetness or more vinegar or liquid smoke for tang.

After cooking, if you find your beans are too watery, press Sauté and simmer until they reach your desired consistency.

Spanish Rice

GLUTEN FREE • SOY FREE • NUT FREE • EGG FREE • VEGETARIAN OPTION

2 tablespoons (28 g) unsalted butter

2 cups (380 g) long-grain white rice

1 medium onion, diced

2 teaspoons (6 g) minced garlic

1¾ cups (411 ml) chicken stock

1 cup (235 ml) tomato sauce

1 tablespoon (8 g) ground cumin

2 teaspoons (6 g) chili powder

1 teaspoon dried oregano

¼ cup (4 g) chopped fresh cilantro

Zest and juice of 1 lime

—

6 servings

Press Sauté on your electric pressure cooker. When the inner pot is hot, add the butter and dry rice. Sauté for 2 minutes.

Stir in the onion and continue to sauté until the onion is translucent, another 2 minutes. Add the garlic and cook an additional 30 seconds, until fragrant. Press Cancel.

Add the chicken stock, tomato sauce, cumin, chili powder, and oregano in with the rice.

Close and lock the lid, making sure the steam release handle is in the sealing position. Cook on high pressure for 12 minutes. When the cook time is finished, allow a 5-minute natural release, then do a quick release to vent any remaining steam. When the float pin drops, unlock the lid and open it carefully.

Transfer to a serving bowl, add the cilantro, lime juice, and lime zest. Fluff the rice with a fork and serve!

NOTE:

To make this rice vegetarian, replace the chicken stock with vegetable stock for an equally delicious option.

Sweet and Easy Corn Bread

GLUTEN FREE • SOY FREE • NUT FREE

⅓ cup (47 g) Bob's Red Mill medium-grind gluten-free yellow cornmeal

1 cup (120 g) Bob's Red Mill Gluten-Free 1-to-1 Baking Mix

1 tablespoon (8 g) baking powder

1 teaspoon salt

¼ cup (56 g) unsalted butter, melted

¼ cup (80 g) honey

½ cup (120 ml) buttermilk

1 large egg

¾ cup (113 g) sweet yellow corn, fresh, frozen, or canned

1 cup (235 ml) water for the bottom of the pot

—

6 servings

NOTE:

This corn bread is best eaten the day you make it, but will keep for several days, well wrapped in the refrigerator.

Spray a 7 x 3-inch (18 x 7.6 cm) cake pan with nonstick cooking spray. Set aside.

In a large bowl, combine all the ingredients until just mixed. Don't overmix the batter. Pour the batter into the prepared pan. Allow the batter to sit for at least 15 minutes before baking. When you're ready to bake, spray a piece of aluminum foil with nonstick cooking spray and cover the pan tightly (spray side down), crimping the edges to seal.

Pour 1 cup (235 ml) water into the inner pot of your pressure cooker. Place a trivet in the pot over the water. Use a foil sling (see page 11) and gently lower the filled pan onto the trivet.

Close and lock the lid, making sure the steam release handle is in the sealing position. Cook on high pressure for 25 minutes. When the cook time is finished, do a quick pressure release by carefully moving the sealing handle to venting and allowing all the steam to escape. When the float pin drops, unlock the lid and open it carefully. Remove the pan from the inner pot. Remove the foil cover and allow the corn bread to cool for 10 minutes before slicing into wedges and serving.

Cheesy Au Gratin Potatoes

GLUTEN FREE • NUT FREE • SOY FREE • VEGETARIAN

2 tablespoons (28 g) unsalted butter

1 medium onion, chopped

2 cloves garlic, minced

1 cup (235 ml) vegetable stock

½ teaspoon salt

¼ teaspoon freshly cracked black pepper

6 medium russet potatoes, peeled and sliced ⅛ inch (3 mm) thick

1 cup (55 g) gluten-free panko bread crumbs

3 tablespoons (45 ml) melted unsalted butter

½ cup (120 g) sour cream

½ cup (60 g) shredded mild cheddar cheese

½ cup (60 g) shredded Gruyère cheese

—

6 servings

Press Sauté or Browning on your electric pressure cooker. When the inner pot is hot, add the 2 tablespoons (28 g) butter. When the butter is melted, add the onion and cook, stirring occasionally, until tender, about 5 minutes. Add the garlic and cook for an additional 30 seconds, until fragrant. Add the stock, salt, and pepper, scraping up any browned bits from the bottom of the pot.

Add a steamer basket to the bottom of your pot over the onion and garlic mixture. Place the sliced potatoes in the basket. Close and lock the lid, making sure the steam release valve is in the sealing position. Cook on high pressure for 7 minutes.

Meanwhile, preheat your broiler and grease a 9 x 13-inch (23 x 33 cm) casserole dish. In a small bowl, combine the panko bread crumbs with the 3 tablespoons (45 ml) melted butter. Set aside.

When the potatoes are finished cooking, use the quick release method by opening the release handle and venting all the steam. When the float pin drops, unlock the lid and open it carefully.

Remove the potatoes and the steamer basket. Place the potatoes into the prepared casserole dish. While the pot is still hot, add the sour cream and both of the cheeses to the cooking liquid in the pressure cooker. Stir until the cheese is melted and smooth.

Carefully pour the cheese sauce over the cooked potatoes and stir gently to combine. Top the potatoes with the bread crumbs. Place under the broiler for 5 to 6 minutes, or until the topping is golden brown.

NOTE:

Use these cheesy potatoes as an accompaniment to our Classic Whole Baked Chicken (page 72), or BBQ Baby Back Ribs (page 83).

Savory Corn Bread

GLUTEN FREE • DAIRY-FREE OPTION • SOY FREE • NUT FREE

1 cup (120 g) brown rice flour (Authentic Foods brand is gluten free and not gritty)

½ cup (60 g) sorghum flour (Bob's Red Mill brand is gluten free)

¾ cup (105 g) plus 2 tablespoons (18 g) medium-grind gluten-free cornmeal, divided

2 teaspoons (5 g) baking powder

½ teaspoon salt

½ teaspoon onion powder

½ teaspoon garlic powder

1 teaspoon psyllium husk powder or ½ teaspoon xanthan gum

1 teaspoon finely chopped fresh thyme

¼ cup (56 g) unsalted butter or dairy-free butter such as Earth Balance

1 cup (235 ml) milk or dairy-free milk

1 egg, lightly beaten

1 cup (235 ml) water

—

4 servings

Spray a 7 x 3-inch (18 x 7.6 cm) cake pan with nonstick cooking spray, then dust with 2 tablespoons (18 g) of the cornmeal. Set aside.

In a large mixing bowl, combine the two flours, remaining ¾ cup (105 g) cornmeal, baking powder, salt, onion and garlic powders, psyllium husk powder, and thyme. Whisk together until thoroughly blended.

In a microwave-safe bowl, melt the butter and whisk into the flour mixture; add the milk and beaten egg. Whisk to combine all of the ingredients and stir until smooth.

Pour into the prepared baking pan and tap lightly on the counter to release any air bubbles. Spray a square of aluminum foil with nonstick cooking spray and place (sprayed side down) over the corn bread mixture.

Add the water to the inner pot of your pressure cooker. Place a trivet in the pot. Using a foil sling (see page 11), carefully lower the covered cake pan into the pot on top of the trivet.

Close and lock the lid, making sure the steam release knob is in the sealing position. Cook on high pressure for 35 minutes. When the cook time is finished, do a quick pressure release by carefully moving the sealing knob to venting and allowing all the steam to escape. When the float pin drops, unlock the lid and open it carefully.

Remove the corn bread from the pot and place on a cooling rack. Remove the foil from the top and let the corn bread cool to room temperature.

"Hits the Spot" Brussels Sprouts

GLUTEN FREE • VEGETARIAN OPTION • SOY FREE • EGG FREE

2 tablespoons (30 ml) olive or vegetable oil

6 strips of gluten-free bacon, chopped (optional)

⅓ cup (79 ml) apple cider vinegar (Braggs brand is gluten free)

¼ cup (60 ml) maple syrup

1 teaspoon ground ginger

1 teaspoon salt

1 teaspoon coarsely ground pepper

2 pounds (907 g) fresh Brussels sprouts, trimmed and cut in half

2 large Fuji apples, peeled, cored, and diced

¼ cup (30 g) dried cranberries

½ cup (58 g) chopped hazelnuts, toasted

¼ cup (38 g) crumbled goat cheese

—

6 servings

Press Sauté on your electric pressure cooker. When the inner pot is hot, add the oil. Add the chopped bacon and cook until crisp and crumbly. Move the bacon to a paper towel–lined plate, but leave the drippings in the pan. Set the bacon aside. Press Cancel.

Add the cider vinegar, maple syrup, ginger, salt, and pepper to the pot and whisk to combine with bacon drippings. Add the Brussels sprouts, apples, and dried cranberries, tossing well to coat.

Close and lock the lid, making sure the steam release knob is closed in the sealing position. Cook on high pressure for 1 minute. When it is finished, use a quick release by opening the release knob and venting the steam. When the float pin drops, unlock the lid and open it carefully.

Serve the Brussels sprouts sprinkled with the reserved bacon, hazelnuts, and crumbled goat cheese.

Green Bean Casserole with Fried Onions

GLUTEN FREE • SOY FREE • NUT FREE

FOR THE GREEN BEANS

2 tablespoons (28 g) unsalted butter

1 large onion, halved and thinly sliced

5 cloves garlic, finely diced

1 pound (454 g) button mushrooms, sliced

1 teaspoon salt

1½ pounds (680 g) fresh green beans

¼ teaspoon ground nutmeg

½ teaspoon red pepper flakes

1 cup (235 ml) vegetable stock

3 tablespoons (34 g) diced roasted red bell peppers

½ cup (120 ml) heavy cream

2 tablespoons (30 ml) cold water (optional)

2 tablespoons (16 g) cornstarch (optional)

FOR THE FRIED ONION TOPPING

Vegetable oil, for frying

3 tablespoons (24 g) tapioca flour

1 teaspoon salt

¼ teaspoon black pepper

1 medium onion, thinly sliced into rings

—

6 servings

GREEN BEANS: Press Sauté on your electric pressure cooker. When the inner pot is hot, add the butter. When the butter has melted, add the onion and cook for 5 minutes, or until softened and just beginning to brown. Add the garlic and cook for an additional 30 seconds, until fragrant.

Add the sliced mushrooms to the onions, sprinkle with the salt, and cook for 3 minutes, stirring occasionally. Press Cancel while you prepare the green beans.

Rinse the green beans under cold water and trim the ends. If the green beans are too long, cut them in half so they will fit into your pressure cooker. Add the green beans, nutmeg, red pepper flakes, and vegetable stock to the mushrooms and onions in the pot. Stir to combine.

Close and lock the lid, making sure the steam release knob is in the sealing position. Cook on high pressure for 1 minute. When it is finished, use a quick release by opening the release knob and venting all the steam. When the float pin drops, unlock the lid and open it carefully.

Add the roasted red bell peppers and heavy cream to the green beans. Stir until well combined. If the mixture is too thin for your liking, make a slurry by mixing the cold water and cornstarch in a small bowl and whisking until the mixture is smooth. Add the slurry to the beans and stir until it thickens. Press Cancel, but return the lid to keep the beans warm. Spray an 8-inch (20.3 cm) casserole dish with nonstick cooking spray and set aside.

FRIED ONION TOPPING: In a medium saucepan, heat 1 inch (2.5 cm) of vegetable oil to 375°F (190°C).

In a bowl, combine the tapioca flour, salt, and pepper. Stir gently to combine. Add the thinly sliced onions and toss with your hands until the onion is well coated with flour.

Very gently shake any excess flour off the onion rings and carefully place a few at a time into the hot oil. Fry the onions in small batches until golden brown and crispy. When they are done, remove the onions from the oil with a slotted spoon and drain them on a paper towel–lined plate.

When all the onions are done cooking, open the lid of your pressure cooker and transfer the green bean mixture to the prepared casserole dish. Spread the fried onions over the green beans and place the dish under the broiler for 3 to 4 minutes, until heated through and crispy on top.

About the Authors

JANE BONACCI *is the founder and author of The Heritage Cook food blog and coauthor of The Gluten-Free Bread Machine Cookbook. She is an expert in gluten-free baking and cooking, as well as a professional food writer and recipe developer, editor, and tester. She lives with her husband in the San Francisco Bay Area.*

SARA DE LEEUW *is a culinary instructor, professional recipe tester/developer, and a freelance writer. She is the founder of the food blog My Imperfect Kitchen, where she shares that while life isn't perfect, it should always be delicious! When not in the kitchen, Sara teaches private cooking classes and hosts live public cooking demos. She lives with her husband near Los Angeles, California.*